# IMPACT

## The Story of the September 11 Terrorist Attacks

BY MATT DOEDEN

**CAPSTONE PRESS**
a capstone imprint

Tangled History is published by Capstone Press,
1710 Roe Crest Drive, North Mankato, Minnesota 56003
www.capstonepub.com

Library of Congress Cataloging-in-Publication Data
Doeden, Matt.
Impact : the story of the September 11 terrorist attacks / by Matt Doeden.
pages cm. — (Tangled history)
Includes bibliographical references and index.
Summary: "In a narrative nonfiction format, follows people who experienced the
events of September 11, 2001"— Provided by publisher.
ISBN 978-1-4914-7079-4 (library binding) — ISBN 978-1-4914-7083-1 (pbk.) —
ISBN 978-1-4914-7087-9 (ebook pdf)
1. September 11 Terrorist Attacks, 2001—Juvenile literature. 2. Terrorism—United
States—Juvenile literature. I. Title.
HV6432.7.D637 2016
973.931—dc23                                              2014048931

Editorial Credits
Jennifer Besel, editor; Tracy Davies McCabe, designer; Tracy Cummins, media
researcher; Tori Abraham, production specialist

Photo Credits
AP Photo: ASSOCIATED PRESS, 52, Tribune Review/Scott Spangler, 76; Corbis: David Turnley, 4,
REUTERS/Sean Adair, 36, REUTERS/Shannon Stapleton, 28, Richard Cohen, 66, Sygma/Neville
Elder, 50, ZUMA Press/Rob Schoenbaum, 82; Getty Images: AFP PHOTO/John G. MABANGLO,
62, Gamma-Rapho/Tammy KLEIN, 86, Joseph Pobereskin, 12, Mario Tama, 44, New York Daily
News Archive/David Handschuh, Cover, NY Daily News Archive/Keith Torrie, 6, Richard Strauss/
Smithsonian, 48, Wirelmage/Jamie McCarthy, 104; Newscom: KRT/DAMON WINTER, 105 Top,
REUTERS/Larry Downing, 54, Splash News/Phil Penman, 105 Bottom; Shutterstock: Anthony
Correia, 20, goir, Design Element, Ken Tannenbaum, 16, Picsfive, Back Cover; Thinkstock: Getty
Images/Alex Wong, 10; Wikimedia: Bob Jagendorf, 103, TSGT Cedric H. Rudisill, USAF, 96.

Print in Canada.
032015    008825FRF15

# TABLE OF CONTENTS

Shock ............................................................ 4

1) One of Those Days ............................................ 6

2) Good Luck ..................................................... 10

3) 73 Floors up ................................................... 12

4) In a Flash ..................................................... 16

5) Not Just Another Day ......................................... 20

6) Behind the Elevator Doors .................................... 28

7) A Second Impact .............................................. 36

8) Race Against Time ............................................ 44

9) Hijacked ...................................................... 50

10) Target Three ................................................. 54

11) Let's Roll .................................................... 62

12) The Unthinkable .............................................. 66

13) No Words ..................................................... 76

14) Four Floors From Freedom .................................... 82

15) Down Comes Another .......................................... 86

16) Daylight ..................................................... 96

Epilogue ........................................................ 102

Timeline ........................................................ 106

Glossary ........................................................ 108

Critical Thinking Using the Common Core ......................... 109

Internet Sites .................................................. 109

Further Reading ................................................. 110

Selected Bibliography ........................................... 110

Index ........................................................... 112

About the Author ............................................... 112

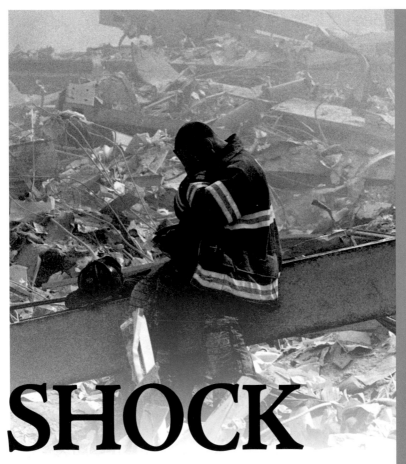

# SHOCK

Early on the morning of September 11, 2001, the United States seemed to be just about the safest place in the world to live. The nation hadn't been attacked on its own soil since the bombing of Pearl Harbor six decades before. War seemed like something that happened elsewhere. Perhaps that, more than anything, is what made the massive terror attacks of that day so shocking.

The U.S. government had seen the warning signs. Threats from terrorist cells in nations such as Afghanistan, Saudi Arabia, and Pakistan, where anti-American sentiments ran hot, were nothing new. But few citizens knew much about those threats.

So when the attack did come, it was so shocking in scale that those who witnessed it could barely believe what was happening. Around the nation and the world, countless viewers sat glued to their TVs, watching the unbelievable events play out in New York City; Washington, D.C.; and a field in Pennsylvania. Four hijacked airplanes. Almost 3,000 people killed. The images viewers saw remain etched in their memories forever.

But the shock of that day for TV viewers was nothing compared to the shock and horror experienced by those who were actually there. The people in this book are real. The events are real. Their stories are real. This is a story about a day full of violence and tragedy. But it's also a story of heroism, triumph, and the will to survive even the most extreme circumstances.

# ONE OF THOSE DAYS

## 1

Newark International Airport

## Mark Bingham

Newark, New Jersey, September 11, 2001, about 7:40 a.m.

"Oh, this is not what I need, Matt."

Mark Bingham was restless in the passenger seat of his friend's car. He glanced down at the clock, then back up at the busy road. His friend Matt weaved in and out of traffic. It was going to be close.

"Don't worry," Matt said with a grin. "You'll make that flight yet. It's right up here—Terminal A." He swung the car into a spot right in front of the terminal, slamming on the brakes. "Get going!"

"Thanks, Matt. Sorry to rush off like this."

With a wave to his friend, Bingham grabbed his bag and hurried into Newark International Airport. He had less than 20 minutes until his flight to San Francisco was scheduled to depart. It would be close, but Bingham was an experienced traveler. If anyone could navigate airport security in time, he was the man. Bingham ducked and dodged his athletic frame through the press of people waiting to get on their planes.

With his duffel bag slung over his broad shoulders and his ticket in hand, Bingham rushed down the concourse toward Gate 17. His heart sank as he saw his gate, the words "United Airlines Flight 93—San Francisco—Now Boarding" lit up above. The waiting area was empty, not a passenger in sight. *Not good*. A United Airlines employee was preparing to shut the gate as he ran up, out of breath.

"Am I too late?" he huffed.

"You cut that one close," said the woman with a smile. "They're just about to shut the aircraft door. You'll be the last one on. Have a nice flight."

The plane was less than half full, Bingham noted as he stepped aboard. Lots of empty seats. That was good. Nothing was worse than a jam-packed airplane, especially on a cross-country flight. Bingham stashed his bag in the overhead compartment and found his seat in the fourth row. A former rugby player, Bingham was built with broad shoulders. A coach seat would always be a tight fit for him, but here in first class there was plenty of room.

"Hey," he said to the man in the seat next to him. "This is me, 4D."

"Hello," said the man with a smile. "Name's Tom. Tom Burnett."

Bingham gave him a firm handshake and a smile, glad to be sitting next to a friendly passenger. It seemed like so many passengers just wanted to close themselves off during a flight. Bingham liked to visit, whether it was with passengers or flight attendants. It helped pass the time. "Well, I guess we'd better get comfortable, Tom. Long flight ahead."

Bingham glanced around the cabin. So many different people. Families, business travelers, tourists. An elderly man was reading the sports section of the newspaper. A young woman was making one last call on her cell phone before shutting it off. A Middle-Eastern young man was just sitting there, looking nervous. *Must be afraid of flying*, Bingham thought with a smile.

A flight attendant brought Bingham an orange juice. He sat back and took a sip as the pilot came over the intercom.

"Sorry, folks, but we've got a delay on the runway. We'll be leaving a little late this morning."

*One of those days*, Bingham thought.

What else can go wrong?

# GOOD LUCK

**2**

Dulles International Airport

It was a lovely Washington, D.C., morning.
The sky was blue and bright. Danielle O'Brien sat
at her station in the flight control tower of Dulles
International Airport. It was a busy weekday
morning, and Danielle gripped her headset as she
tracked the local air traffic on her screen.

"American Airlines Flight 77, climb and
maintain 5,000 feet," she said. The big Boeing
757 climbed into the sky, bound for Los Angeles.
O'Brien tracked the blip that represented Flight 77
and made a quick adjustment, ordering the airplane
to climb to 11,000 feet.

"Good luck," she told the pilot as the airplane
left Washington's airspace. O'Brien was already on
to the next flight under her control. Planes came
and went all day. Flight 77 was off to California.
She never expected to see it again.

But O'Brien had not seen the last of Flight 77
that day. Flight 77 was coming back, and because
of it, life would never be the same.

**3**

# 73 FLOORS UP

The twin towers of the World Trade
Center dominated the New York skyline.

# Nicole Simpson

South Tower of the World Trade
Center in New York City, 8:21 a.m.

The streets of New York City were
crowded. People coming and going.
Cabs picking up and dropping off.
The sidewalks a sea of people. Nicole
Simpson loved it. Earlier that morning
she had run her fingers through her long
dark hair as she looked up at the south
tower of the World Trade Center. One-
hundred ten stories—just like its twin,
the north tower. The towers gleamed
against a bright blue sky. It was going to
be a beautiful day.

Life was busy. A mother of two, Simpson was a financial adviser at Morgan Stanley. She had casually made her way up to her 73rd-floor office, grabbing a cup of coffee along the way. She was one of the first in the office, and spent the early morning hours preparing for the rest of her day.

Simpson called her small group of assistants into a meeting to plan out their day. "We've got a lot on our plate this morning," she explained. "First, we need to …"

*Suddenly, the building shook. It felt like everything was moving. The floor, the walls, the ceiling. Everything was swaying back and forth.*

Simpson instinctively threw her arms out to steady herself. An earthquake? New York City didn't have earthquakes!

The looks on the faces of everyone else in the room mirrored what she was feeling. None of them had ever felt anything quite like it.

"What was that?" asked one young woman who was nervously tapping her pen on the conference table. There was an edge of panic in her voice.

"Oh God, was it another bomb?" asked another. "We should get out."

Everyone who worked in the World Trade Center knew that terrorists had bombed the building before. But that had been underground. They were 73 floors up. To feel a bomb way up here … was that even possible? Simpson had no idea, but she wasn't about to jump to conclusions. The last thing she wanted was a panic.

She was about to tell everyone to calm down. But before she got a chance to open her mouth, she glanced out the window. Outside, the New York City skyline was a familiar scene. She'd seen it a thousand times. But this was a view unlike any she'd seen before. Outside, hundreds of feet above the streets below, she saw paper everywhere. It was floating down from above, reminding her of a ticker-tape parade the city had held after the Yankees won the World Series.

Only this was no parade. This paper was on fire.

# IN A FLASH

**4**

A woman sits at her desk on the 93rd floor of the World Trade Center's north tower. She rubs her temples as she looks at the spreadsheet before her. By chance she glances up, out her window.

Her last moments are filled with terror. An airplane. An explosion. A scream cut short.

He is on the 99th floor, tapping away at a keyboard, trying to set up his company's new e-mail server, when he hears it … feels it. The building shakes. The computer monitor blinks off. The lights flicker. He hears screams.

He rushes into the hallway. Smoke begins to pour in. The shrill piercing of the smoke detectors rings in his ears.

The smoke grows thicker. There is nowhere to run. He drops to his hands and knees, gasping for air. But there is none. He crawls, blind, searching for refuge, for escape.

He coughs, dizzy and confused. Temperature rising. The crackle of flames. He shouts in a choked voice … "Help!"

But no one comes.

---

She is crying. There's nowhere to go. Thick black smoke fills the small office. She opens a window, sticks her head out just for the clean air.

Then the flames come. They rise up from the floor below. Hotter, hotter, hotter. Within minutes, it's unbearable. She's roasting alive. Trapped.

She has no choice. She has to get out. She throws the window open the rest of the way.

She jumps.

---

He is in the stairwell when it happens. His ears ring from the massive explosion. He lifts a hand to his face and feels blood trickling from his forehead.

He has to get out. Something terrible is happening. He bounds down the stairs. Behind him, flames and smoke. He runs down … down … down. Two steps at a time. Three steps. Floor by floor. The smoke thins. The flames are behind him. Soon there are others fleeing.

Down, down, down. All he wants is to get out.

# NOT JUST ANOTHER DAY

**5**

New York City firefighters battled the blaze at what became known as Ground Zero.

# Jan Demczur

Jan Demczur didn't understand what was happening. Neither did the five other men in the elevator with him.

Just a few moments before, Demczur had been hard at work cleaning the windows on the 44th floor of the World Trade Center's north tower. Being a window washer in one of the world's biggest skyscrapers was quite a task. It was a never-ending battle against dust and smudges. Nothing beat the satisfaction of a job well done.

Demczur had been on his way up to the 74th floor to carry on that battle when it happened. One moment he and the others had been standing in the elevator, quietly staring forward, each man minding his own business in a textbook display of elevator etiquette. Then the next, they all heard a sound —a deep, powerful THUD! It was a low, muffled, drawn-out sound, but it came with shocking intensity. *Demczur could feel it through his feet, his legs, his whole body. He didn't know what it was. But it was big, and it was bad.*

The elevator swayed from side to side, creaking on its rigid cables.

Demczur instinctively threw out his arms to catch his balance. The other men did the same, looks of confusion written across their faces. The time for polite elevator etiquette was over. Something was happening outside.

One neatly dressed man was clutching a container of milk he'd just purchased. "This isn't good," he said with a frown.

The elevator was deadly silent for a moment. It hung there, very slowly swaying. The ominous creaking of the cables had Demczur holding his breath.

The creaking stopped with the loud pop of a snapping cable. Then the floor of the elevator seemed to fall out from under their feet as the car plummeted down. Demczur lunged forward, pounding on the elevator's emergency stop button. The elevator noisily ground to a halt. Its lights flickered and dimmed. To one side, a man cursed.

Moments later, a voice spoke over the building's intercom. "There has been an explosion. Please proceed to the nearest exit."

That was all. *An explosion*. What did that mean? An accident with a gas line? A bomb? The men waited in silence for more information, but none came. All Demczur could hear was the heavy breathing of the five other men. They were all thinking the same thing. Finally, the man with the milk said it out loud.

"We're trapped."

That was when the smoke began oozing into the elevator.

"What was that?"

Jay Jonas, captain of Ladder Company 6 of New York City's fire department, looked at several of his men across the table. Each of the men sat frozen, several with coffee cups in hand. They'd all heard it. A loud buzzing, like a low-flying airplane. Then a massive boom. Whatever that was, it was big and it was close.

Jonas led them as they rushed outside the fire station. What they saw was madness. Debris rained down onto the streets from the nearby World Trade Center. "A plane just crashed!" said one of the firefighters, pointing to the sky. "A plane just crashed into the World Trade Center!"

It seemed hard to believe, but the proof was all around him. Glass and metal were falling like rain. Not 20 feet from the firehouse, a computer monitor smashed into the street and broke into a thousand pieces.

"What kind of plane?" Jonas asked. He was trying to picture it. Maybe a small two-seater prop plane? Some little crop duster?

"A big one ... a commercial jet."

Jonas was a veteran firefighter. Sometimes he felt like he'd seen it all. But he'd never seen anything like this. Had never even heard of anything like it. A commercial jet crash and a high-rise fire all at once?

"Company, turn out!" Jonas shouted. His men were already on the move. "Get your gear on. Go! Go! Go!"

His men were all experienced firefighters, and they wasted no time getting geared up and loading their engine, even as the world outside seemed to be crashing down around them. Firefighting veterans Matt Komorowski and Tommy Falco were already in their black and yellow FDNY gear. Jonas helped the powerfully built Bill Butler hoist heavy gear up onto the engine. A dozen men working together like a well-oiled machine. He heard distant sirens wailing—other companies on their way.

Debris continued to fall all around them. But the real horror was above. Jonas craned his neck and looked up. There it was. A gash in the side of the north tower. Bright orange flames. Thick black smoke.

The emergency bands on Jonas' radio lit up as frantic reports came in from firefighters, police officers, and other emergency workers. "Emergency crews to 1 World Trade Center … massive fireball … reports of a low-flying aircraft, possibly a 737 … all units report …"

How was that even possible? Jonas couldn't stop trying to make sense of the disaster unfolding right in front of him. He shook his head. How didn't matter right now. All that mattered was that lives were in danger. Flames licked the outside of the north tower, and the blaze was quickly spreading. Already, at least 20 floors of the skyscraper were burning.

And that was no ordinary fire. A commercial jet would be carrying jet fuel. That fuel would cause a flame that would burn hotter and spread faster than anything he and his men were used to battling. *How was anyone supposed to fight a fire that big, that hot, all more than 70 stories above the ground?*

"Ready, Captain," said Komorowski. "Let's go!"

The siren wailed as the fire engine rolled into action. The scene on the ground was almost as horrifying as the one in the sky. Streams of panicked people poured out of both towers, as well as the surrounding buildings. The engine had to weave slowly through the masses of people on its way to Vesey Street, where the north tower stood.

Debris was everywhere—glass, metal, paper. As Jonas took it all in, he heard a piercing scream. A woman was pointing up at one of the high floors, where the flames were an inferno. Jonas caught the shape of a body falling from the tower.

"Someone just jumped!" said Komorowski. "They're jumping out of the windows! Oh no, no!"

It was horrifying. Jonas couldn't let himself dwell on the horror, however. There was a fire to fight. There were people who needed saving.

"OK, ready, set, go," he shouted to his men. And while everyone else was desperately trying to get out of the burning tower, Ladder Company 6 was going in.

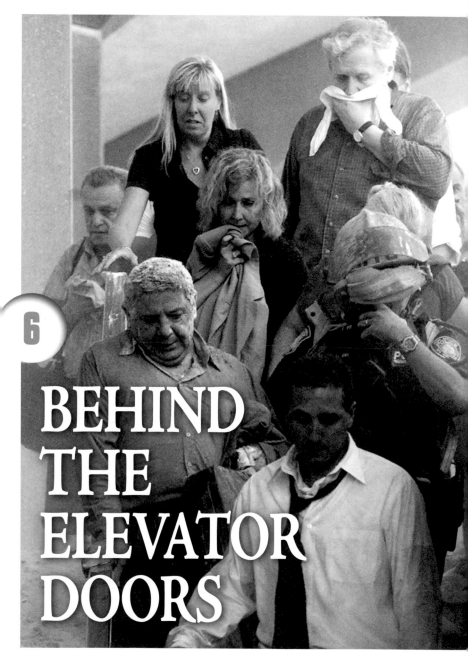

# 6

# BEHIND THE ELEVATOR DOORS

Covered in dust and ash, survivors escaped the burning towers by rushing down the stairwells.

As smoke rolled into the closed elevator car, the man with the milk— George Phoenix—was searching for a ceiling hatch.

Jan Demczur had another idea. "Help me with the doors," he told several of the others.

Together the men pried open the elevator doors. Just a crack at first, but they kept at it. Demczur stuck the wooden handle of one of his squeegees between the two sliding panels to prop them open. He hoped they could peek through to one of the floors. But they weren't that lucky. All they could see on the other side of the door was a solid wall with the number 50 stenciled on it.

"This elevator doesn't service the 50th floor," Phoenix said. "There's no exit here!"

Demczur ran his fingers over the wall. "This is just drywall," he said. "We could break through it. Drywall panels are just an inch thick, not that strong. Does anyone have a knife?" No one did. Not a single blade among them.

"We just need something sharp, something metal," Phoenix said. "There's got to be something!"

The men dug through their pockets, sifting through pens, keys, and anything else they could find. But the walls might as well have been brick for all the good those tools would have done.

And then Demczur had it. His squeegees had metal edges. He grabbed one and rubbed the blade back and forth over the drywall. It was a poor tool for the job, but slowly he began to carve a dent. It was time-consuming, exhausting work. The smoke was growing thicker and thicker. Phoenix and the other men covered their noses and mouths with handkerchiefs just to breathe.

"Here, let me," said Phoenix, taking the tool and attacking the wall with new energy. For the next few minutes the men took turns with the blade. Each hacked away with everything he had, then he turned it over to the next man in a race against time

Soon it was Demczur's turn again. They'd cut through one panel, then another behind that one. Demczur was working on a third panel of drywall when he lost his grip on the squeegee.

For a moment the elevator car was silent. All Demczur could hear was the clanging of the squeegee as it tumbled down the elevator shaft below.

# Nicole Simpson

As Nicole Simpson watched a cloud of burning paper slowly descend to the streets below, she felt a cold knot forming in the pit of her stomach. "Let's go," she told her coworkers. Moments ago, she had been trying to remain calm, trying not to overreact. No longer. "Now!"

They rushed out into the hallway where people were staring out the windows, buzzing about what was happening and what to do next. To Simpson's dismay, many didn't share her urgency to get out of the building.

"The explosion was in the north tower," one man said. "It shouldn't affect us here in the south tower. We should be safe."

Simpson disagreed. She didn't feel safe at all. Her heart was racing, her hands trembling. Nobody really understood what was happening, and she wasn't about to take any chances. She wanted to get out of the building as quickly as she could. As she rounded a corner and marched toward the elevators, she saw that she wasn't alone in that desire. An ever-growing crowd was gathered in front of the elevators, waiting for the doors to open.

Hundreds—maybe thousands—of people would be trying to get onto the elevators, both above and below. They could be waiting for hours. "The stairs," she told her colleagues, leading her team past the elevator doors and into the stairwell.

"Move quickly but safely," she said, leading the way. They were far from alone. A stream of people was fleeing down the stairwell. A man in a dark suit nodded to Simpson. His skin was pale white, as if the blood had drained from his face.

"Does anyone know what's going on?" she asked. "They said it was an explosion."

"It was an airplane," the man said. His voice was trembling. "I saw it. I saw it myself out of my office window. It was a big commercial airliner. It slammed right into the building. You can't imagine it. You can't

... *I'll never forget the sight as long as I live.*"

"An airplane? But it's perfectly clear outside. A bright, sunny day? How could an accident like that happen?"

"I ... I can't say. I don't know. But to me it looked ... it looked intentional."

Intentional? What kind of maniac would purposely fly an airplane into a skyscraper? It was almost impossible to even consider. Yet the weather was good and visibility was high. How else could she explain it?

Simpson's mind raced as they descended. Down, down, down the stairs they went. Floor after floor. Hurried, but orderly. She silently prayed and found a sort of strange calm in the act.

Then a voice came over the building's public address system. "The building is secure," the voice said. "There is no need to evacuate."

"Thank goodness," said the man in the dark suit. "I'm not sure I could do many more stairs. Let's find an elevator."

The group exited the stairwell. A large bank of elevators stood before them. Simpson pressed the up button, even though she still felt the urge to leave the building. The doors opened, and people began crowding inside. Simpson was one of the last to get on. As her finger hovered over the button marked 73, she hesitated.

*This feels wrong*, she thought. Her finger hung there in the air several moments more. She looked to her left, then to her right. Everyone else seemed to be relieved, comforted by the announcement. Yet the thought of those elevator doors closing on her filled her with dread. She felt trapped. Almost panicked.

At the last second, Simpson stepped out of the elevator. Her assistants got off with her. She couldn't say exactly why she'd done it. But there she stood, watching the doors close on the faces of friends, coworkers, strangers.

She'd never see their faces again.

# A SECOND IMPACT

**7**

South Tower, 9:03 a.m.

Around the nation people watched in horror as reporters broadcast the tragic scene at the north tower. For many the images on their TV sets were almost too much to take in.

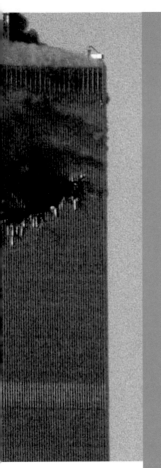

Photographers captured the scene as United Flight 175 flew into the south tower.

On one station the news coverage switched to a view from a distant camera. The shot showed a larger part of the New York skyline with one of the Twin Towers engulfed in flames, smoke oozing from an open gash in the side of the building.

It all seemed horrible, terrible, and unthinkable. But then, in a heartbeat, it got much, much worse. Countless millions gasped as they watched a dark shape race across the screen. It seemed more like a Hollywood special effect than real life. It seemed somehow staged, somehow fake. But it was all too real.

It was another airplane. And it had just rammed straight into the other tower.

The lobby of the north tower was in chaos. Jay Jonas, his gear slung over his shoulder, watched as people streamed out of the stairwells. Two badly burned men lay on the floor near the main doors. People were crying. Screaming. Nobody knew what was happening.

Every instinct told Jonas to stop and help the injured men. Helping people was his job, and these men were in bad shape. But he couldn't do that. Not right now. Emergency medical technicians would be on site in moments. Right now Jonas had to worry about the thousands of people trapped in the building above. Still, running by those men was a gut-wrenching decision.

Jonas turned back toward the building's main doors as he waved his men along. Outside he could see the shiny windows of the World Financial Center across the street. Suddenly, a bright flash reflected in those windows. Then came a thunderous BOOM!

Outside more glass crashed down onto the street. Jonas and his men gasped as a huge piece of metal slammed into the ground. A man ran into the lobby from the street. "A second plane," said the breathless man. "A second plane just hit the other tower!"

*Not again!* Jonas thought. One massive fire was almost more than he could imagine fighting. Now there would be two … maybe more. Was this just the beginning? Were there more attacks to come?

Jonas turned to Gerry Nervins, a friend from another company. Nervins' expression was dark. *"We're going to be lucky if we survive this,"* he said. From the eerie silence that filled the lobby for the next several moments, Jonas knew that Nervins wasn't the only one having that same thought.

"What now?" asked Tommy Falco. He and the others were looking to Jonas for orders. None of them had ever seen anything like this. It was time for Jonas to step up and lead.

"So here's the deal," he said, pointing toward Stairwell B, knowing that he might be ordering his men to their deaths. "We gotta walk up 80 floors. And it's a raw deal. I know it's bad, but this is what we're doing."

Not one of the men protested. They nodded, determination written in their faces. "OK, Captain," they agreed. "Let's go. We're with you."

The whole building shook beneath Nicole Simpson's feet. She felt the blast as much as she heard it. In the distance a scream echoed through the hallway.

Then came another crash. Much closer. It took her a moment to realize that she was hearing the sound of the elevator crashing down before her. The same elevator she'd just exited. And it was falling. Crashing. *Oh God …*

She was shaking. Her mind raced. *Now what?*

There was no time to dwell on it. Now both towers were in flames. There were no more doubts in her mind. She had to move. Simpson rushed back into the stairwell, down, down, down, flight after flight. Yet as Simpson continued her descent, she marveled that others were actually climbing up the stairs. Police officers. Firefighters. As desperate as she was to get out, they were climbing up, looking to help. At that moment she felt very proud of her fellow New Yorkers.

Still, Simpson wanted nothing more than to get out, to escape whatever it was that was happening here. The stairwell was crowded, but everyone kept moving. Down, down. Five floors to go ... three ... one. Simpson was breathing heavily. Her panic was growing as she imagined flames, smoke, bombs going off. But she kept it together, smoothing her blouse as she climbed down, trying her best to remain calm, trying not to think about all those people ...

And then, finally, daylight. Simpson breathed deeply as she exited the tower. She stepped out into the air and into chaos all around. The ground was covered with debris. People were running, screaming. Sirens wailing. Paramedics were tending to the injured, the burned. It was like a scene out of a war movie.

Her hands trembled, but her legs were steady. She walked quickly but calmly through the sea of people. She didn't care where she went, only that she got as far away as she could. She crossed Church Street and its masses of people and just kept going. She didn't turn back until she hit Broadway, several blocks from the building.

When she finally allowed herself a moment to rest, to see what had happened, she nearly collapsed. It was horrible. Terrible. Awful. None of the words seemed enough. She had survived. She was out. But life would never be the same.

# RACE AGAINST TIME

**8**

As smoke rose from the collapsed tower, firefighters and survivors could only stand by and watch helplessly.

# Jay Jonas

Jay Jonas and his team were headed up. He didn't know what he'd find there. He'd battled countless fires in his life. But nothing like this.

*One step at a time.*

It was a narrow stairwell, just wide enough for a row of firefighters going up and a row of people going down.

"One of the biggest buildings in the world, and there's one tiny staircase to the ground?" mumbled Tommy Falco. "What were they thinking when they built this place?

Jonas watched as people streamed down. Office workers, custodial employees, tourists. He was proud as he watched them, calm, orderly. People were hurrying, but few were panicked. Jonas and his men gave them all the same message—get out as quickly as you can. Many nodded at them, thanked them, or wished them luck. Some even handed them bottles of water. At that moment—in a packed stairwell amidst a major catastrophe—Jonas swelled with pride for these people.

"Slow and steady," Jonas told his men. "Ten floors, then we take a breather." Already, his radio had piped up with mayday messages for firefighters battling chest pains. Rushing up 80 flights of stairs carrying 100 pounds of gear just wasn't realistic. Jonas had to make sure his men had some energy left when they made it to the fire. If they made it.

"No!" shouted George Phoenix
as the sound of the falling squeegee
clanged down the elevator shaft.
Another man doubled over, coughing
from the ever-thickening smoke. Time
was getting very short. Soon none of
them would be able to breathe, much
less work.

Phoenix stepped forward. He
began pounding the drywall with his
fists and kicking it with his feet. Panic
was setting in. But Jan Demczur
remained calm. He had another
squeegee handle. He grabbed it and
dug right back in on the wall. Within
minutes they were through the third
and final layer of drywall.

All that remained was a layer of white tiles. With their fists and feet, the six men broke through that last layer. The sound of tile crashing to the floor was music to Demczur's ears. They were through!

"It's a bathroom," Phoenix shouted. "Keep going!"

The men relentlessly cut and pounded on the walls, carving out a wider and wider opening. Soon the hole was just big enough. One by one, they squeezed themselves through the small opening. Demczur reached back through the opening to grab his bucket.

The National Museum of American History now houses Demczur's squeegee as part of a collection of September 11 artifacts.

"Really?" asked Phoenix. "You're taking that?"

"Of course," Demczur answered. "The company I work for might not get me another one."

In spite of everything that was happening, in spite of the explosion, the smoke, the frantic effort to escape the doomed elevator, the men laughed. And so, with his bucket in hand, Demczur and the others ran out into the hallway.

Except for a few firefighters, who were startled to see the ragtag group, the 50th floor was deserted.

# HIJACKED

**9**

Investigators looked through the wreckage after
Flight 93 crashed in Pennsylvania.

# Mark Bingham

It had been a late start, but Flight 93 was on its way. Mark Bingham sat back in his seat, thumbing though the in-flight magazine. Next to him Tom Burnett glanced out the window. The flight attendants were just about to start the food service.

At first when Bingham noticed movement behind him, he didn't think much of it. The seat belt sign was turned off, so people were moving about the cabin, using the restrooms, stretching their legs. Nothing unusual about that.

But as he looked over his shoulder, Bingham saw that there was indeed something unusual going on. Several men were marching together toward the cockpit. Bingham's gaze locked on one of the men, the Middle-Eastern man who Bingham had thought looked nervous before takeoff. Now that man wore a red bandanna on his head. In his hand he grasped a sharp blade. It looked like a box cutter.

Bingham's heart raced as he realized that he was witnessing a hijacking. The moments that followed were a blur. Passengers screaming. Someone shouting there was a bomb on the airplane. A flight attendant brutally stabbed. Crashing noises. A sudden banking and short, sharp descent.

"Everyone to the back of the plane," shouted one of the men in a thick Middle-Eastern accent. "No one has to be hurt. We are taking control of the plane. Remain calm and do not resist, and everyone will go home safe."

Some of the passengers and crew on Flight 93:

Todd Beamer

Alan Beaven

Mark K. Bingham

Deora Frances Bodley

It was mass confusion. The men held some passengers in the front of the plane, while Bingham, Burnett, and a few others were ordered to the back. As they huddled in the back, Bingham looked at Burnett. They exchanged a look that made it clear they were thinking the same thing.

Part of Bingham wanted to act now, to try to overpower these hijackers. But another part of him wanted to follow directions, to just hope they'd all get out of this alive. The hijackers had already attacked at least one person. They wouldn't hesitate to kill him. Still … there was a plane full of able-bodied passengers and just a few hijackers. Could they overwhelm the men with sheer numbers?

Bingham looked at the man in the red bandanna. Then he looked back at Burnett. Burnett shook his head. *Not yet.*

Sandra W. Bradshaw

Thomas E. Burnett

Jason Dahl

Joseph Deluca

# TARGET THREE

## 10

Air traffic control at Dulles
International Airport

# Danielle O'Brien

Dulles International Airport,
Washington D.C., 9:35 a.m.

The control tower was buzzing.
Two airplane attacks in New York
City had air traffic controllers
around the nation scrambling to
land every civilian plane in the sky.
Danielle O'Brien and her coworkers
were tasked with something they'd
never done before—clearing
Washington's airspace entirely.

It was a hurried, yet orderly,
process. The air controllers worked
together, guiding one plane after the
next toward the runway. Slowly, the
blips on her screen faded. Fewer and
fewer aircraft remained in the sky.
The same thing was happening at
airports across the nation.

She blinked as she leaned in closer to her screen. "What is this?"

On her screen she tracked an airplane moving more than 500 miles per hour and flying very low. Commercial airliners just didn't do that.

"Is it a military flight?" she asked Tom Howell, the controller sitting next to her.

Howell leaned in, his brow furrowing as he watched. The plane was 10 miles away. Nine. Closing and dropping quickly.

"That thing is headed toward P-56," O'Brien said. She was right. P-56, short for prohibited area 56, was directly over the heart of Washington, D.C., and was strictly off limits to civilian aircraft.

*"Oh my God," Howell gasped. "It looks like he's headed to the White House!"*

"Five miles," O'Brien counted, her voice shaking. In the background she could hear one of her supervisors on the telephone, desperately trying to send a warning. "Four."

But just before she counted off three, the airplane turned. A sense of relief washed over O'Brien. The controllers in the room let out a collective breath. *It must be a military plane sent to protect the president,* O'Brien thought.

But the plane kept turning and turning … and dropping. It was making a complete 360-degree circle, falling closer and closer to the ground. O'Brien's heart began to race once again.

Then the signal dropped off the screen altogether. The room fell silent. O'Brien was shaking as she waited … waited … waited.

Moments later, the announcement came over the speakers. "The Pentagon's been hit."

# Karen Baker

"I have a feeling it's going to be a long day," said Karen Baker, a media relations specialist working at the Pentagon. She walked with her friend, Elaine Kanellis, through the hallways of the Pentagon, sipping a cup of coffee.

They had seen the devastation of the airplane crashes in New York City. Like Americans all over the country, they had watched with shock and horror as the second plane hit, as the buildings burned and people flung themselves from the upper floors. It was awful.

Then the ground shook. A long, grinding thud rang through the halls. In the distance a voice shouted, "It's a bomb!"

Baker dropped her coffee. She grabbed Kanellis, who was nine months pregnant, by the arm. "Move!"

Everyone in the building had the same idea. The hallways were filled with confusion, though there was very little panic. Nobody could truly be prepared for this, but many Pentagon workers were former military officers. All were educated. They understood how to evacuate in an orderly fashion.

Baker and Kanellis clung to each other as they moved through the crowded hall. Nothing made sense. First the Twin Towers and now the Pentagon? Was this just the beginning?

"My God, what's happening?" Kanellis asked, stumbling. Baker was right there to make sure her friend didn't fall. But she didn't have an answer to Kanellis' question. It could be a bomb. It could be another airplane attack. The building could be on fire. She just didn't know, and that made everything all the more terrifying. All she knew at that moment was that she had to get her friend to safety.

Ahead, a guard was directing people along evacuation routes. "We have to get out," he said. But when their group reached the exit, guards blocked their way.

"She's pregnant. Please let me get her out of here," Baker begged. Kanellis was tiring quickly, leaning on her for support.

"I'm sorry," said the guard. "This exit isn't safe. Move along to the next one."

The hallways were growing more crowded. But through the mass of people came a man driving a cart. The small vehicles were common at the Pentagon. It was exactly what Baker needed.

"Stop!" Baker shouted.

A woman dressed in a U.S. Navy uniform stepped in front of the cart, forcing it to stop. "Get on!" she said, helping Kanellis onto the cart.

"No! Stop!" Kanellis said. "I'm not going anywhere without Karen."

The cart's driver wasn't about to argue with a woman who was clearly in such an advanced stage of pregnancy. "Get on," he said, waving Baker onto the cart. And just like that, they were off.

As they weaved through the crowded halls of the Pentagon, Baker grabbed her cell phone. But the lines were all busy. She couldn't get through. That worried her. Nobody seemed to know what was happening.

The driver zigged and zagged as people made room for it to pass. Finally, the cart reached the exit. Baker looked back as they cleared the building. Smoke billowed out of the west side.

"It was a plane, just like in New York," she overheard. "They're evacuating the White House, Camp David, anything else that could be a target. Nobody knows how many more planes could be up there!"

The area of impact looked bad. But the majority of the building stood undamaged. This attack would not be nearly as deadly as those in New York, Baker realized with relief.

"Come on," she told Kanellis. "Let's get you home."

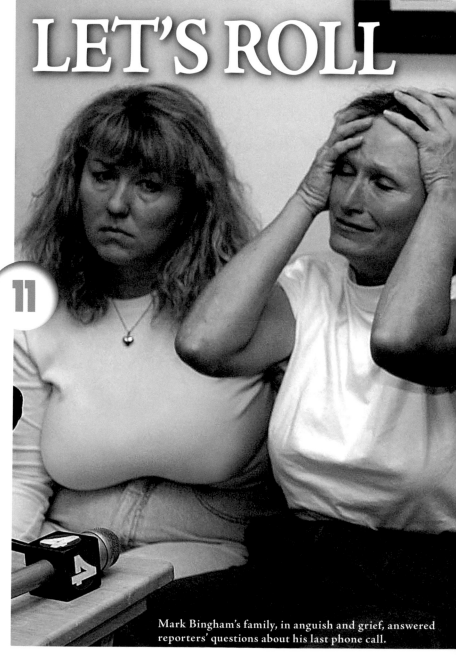

# LET'S ROLL

11

Mark Bingham's family, in anguish and grief, answered reporters' questions about his last phone call.

# Mark Bingham

Flight 93, somewhere over
Pennsylvania, 9:57 a.m.

Mark Bingham kept his eyes open. He was huddled at the back of the plane with nine other passengers and five flight attendants. The rest of the passengers were gathered near the front of the plane in first class. Perhaps the hijackers thought that he and the nine others were the most likely to try to stop them and wanted them as far from the cockpit as possible.

In that, at least, they were right. Bingham and the others had used their cell phones and the airplane's in-flight phones to talk to family members on the ground. And they'd all heard the same story of terrorists hijacking planes and flying them into buildings.

There wasn't a doubt in anyone's mind. The same thing was happening here. But Bingham and the others weren't about to just sit and let it happen.

Bingham glanced over at Todd Beamer. Beamer, a young father, returned the glance and gave a slight nod. It was the signal. Bingham turned and pointed to a flight attendant. The plan was going forward. The attendant calmly turned and headed back to the plane's kitchen area to begin boiling water. Beamer's plan was simple. They would storm the terrorists using the only weapon they could get—scalding hot water.

Beamer was speaking on one of the in-flight phones, describing their dire situation to the operator on the other end. "We've got hijackers with knives," he was saying. "One seems to have a bomb. I don't know where the pilot or copilot are. They may be dead or wounded."

Beamer set down the phone. He looked at Bingham and Tom Burnett. All three men nodded. It was time. Bingham was prepared to do whatever it took to make sure these hijackers failed, even if it meant driving the plane into the ground. He could see by the steel in the others' eyes that they felt the same way.

Beamer stood and led the charge. "Let's roll."

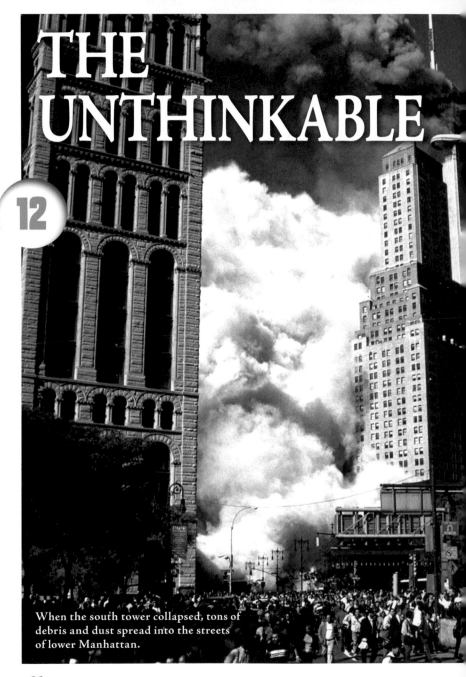

# THE UNTHINKABLE

## 12

When the south tower collapsed, tons of debris and dust spread into the streets of lower Manhattan.

# Rick Leventhal

Rick Leventhal had covered a lot of stories
in his career. But the Fox News reporter had
never seen anything like this. A full-scale
act of war on American soil. He took a deep
breath. He was a professional. He had to
suppress his emotions. He couldn't allow the
fear and rage rolling inside him to surface. His
job was to show America and the world what
was happening.

It had been a battle just to get to the site.
The streets were thick with people fleeing the
burning skyscrapers. But Leventhal and his
engineer, Pat Butler, had fought through the
traffic to get as close as they could.

It was madness. Leventhal was grabbing
people off the streets, doing quick walking
interviews with those who had witnessed
everything firsthand. He was the first TV
reporter to go live at the scene.

67

"I saw it, the first plane," said one man. He was covered in dust. Leventhal walked with him as he moved away from the towers. "It was like something out of a movie. It just slammed right into the building."

And the man walked off. Leventhal was on to the next interview and the next. He would document as much as he could.

Butler waved a hand in his direction. "Get ready, Rick. The network wants us to go live in one minute."

But before they could even set up for the report, they heard a sudden shouting. The earth shook. A low rumble, like thunder, echoed through the streets. A huge cloud of dust began rising up into the sky … a mushroom cloud, like one might see after a nuclear explosion. And it was moving straight toward them. People stampeded down the streets. Ordinary civilians, police officers, first responders. Leventhal shuddered as he saw a young mother with a baby carriage. All running away from that terrible, rapidly expanding cloud.

Leventhal turned to Butler. They locked gazes for a moment. The enormity of what was happening began to dawn on them. The south tower was collapsing.

*"Run!"*

The wall of dust and debris spread out in great plumes, billowing clouds of crushed glass, concrete, bits of metal. It towered over everything and everyone. Screams echoed down the streets. People ran, ducking behind buildings, doing anything they could to get out of the way of that cloud.

Leventhal and Butler sprinted to their news van parked nearby and threw open the door. They dove inside with just moments to spare. Leventhal could only watch as the terrible cloud raced toward them, swallowing everything in its path. And then, everything went dark.

"My God," Butler whispered. "The whole thing, just … gone. How many people were still inside?"

It was horror Leventhal knew he'd never forget. And he knew that it might not be over. The north tower still stood.

Floor by floor, they climbed. Ten floors up … 15 … 20. Jay Jonas stopped his men on the 27th floor for a breather. He was kneeling, sipping on a water bottle, when it happened.

The building swayed. The lights flickered. The floor beneath his feet shook. A loud roar shook the building. It felt like an earthquake, but it went on and on. It seemed like it would never stop.

This was no earthquake.

For a moment everyone was silent. "Check the windows," Jonas said. At first he feared another airplane had struck the building. But this was too loud. The roar had gone on far too long.

Billy Burke, a firefighter from another company, rushed back from a window on the south side of the tower.

"Was that what I thought it was?" Jonas asked, knowing that he didn't want to hear the answer.

Burke's expression gave him the answer even before he spoke the words. "The south tower just collapsed."

The words hung in the air. The silence was deafening as each man tried to grasp the enormity of it. Jonas could hardly believe it. He couldn't even imagine the devastation.

The north tower had been hit first. If the south tower had collapsed, how much longer would the north continue to stand? They were still more than 50 floors from reaching the heart of the blaze. There was no chance.

"OK," he said. "It's time for us to go home. It's time for us to leave."

One of his men began to dump his equipment. "No," Jonas said. "Bring it. You never know what we might need. Bring everything."

Soon after they started back down, Jonas got the official order to evacuate. He was thinking about all the firefighters above them when they rounded a corner somewhere near the 20th floor. There he saw a woman in a doorway. She was just sitting there, crying.

"What's your name?" asked Bill Butler, one of the company's biggest, strongest men.

"Josephine Harris," she answered. She was middle aged and not in the best shape. Her legs had given out from exhaustion, and she could not continue down the stairs on her own.

"Josephine," Butler said putting an arm around her to support her weight, "we're going to get you out of here today."

Harris did her best to move as she leaned on Butler. One foot at a time. Step. Step. Painfully slow. But even this effort was straining her to her limit. "Go," she told them. "Get out. Leave me here."

"Josephine," said Butler. "Your kids and your grandkids want you home today. We gotta keep moving."

Nobody said a word, but Jonas knew they were all thinking it. The clock was ticking. *Faster! We need to move faster!*

Jan Demczur was still clinging to his bucket as he hurried down the stairwell of the north tower. The stairwell was narrow and crowded, but he and the others from the elevator moved down, down, down.

He was on the 11th floor when the south tower collapsed. Or maybe he was on the 12th or 15th … it was hard to remember. Everyone could hear it, feel it, although no one was sure exactly what had happened. Was it another attack? There was nothing to do but continue down.

By the time he reached the third floor, the smoke and dust in the stairway shrouded everything in darkness and made breathing difficult.

Behind him a man doubled over, coughing. People were clinging to one another just to find their next step, piling out into the third floor hallways.

A firefighter, spotting Demczur's maintenance uniform, grabbed him by the arm. "How do we get out?" he asked.

Demczur pointed and the firefighters shined their flashlights down the hallways. *There!* They all saw it. Another staircase. "Go!" shouted one of the firefighters. Demczur opened the door and held it as others streamed through, searching for safety. One of the firefighters grabbed him by the arm and dragged him through into the stairwell. Moments later he was outside.

# NO WORDS

**13**

The impact of Flight 93 left a surprisingly small crater. Rescuers couldn't believe an airplane had crashed there.

It came down fast and steep in the woods of Somerset County, Pennsylvania. At more than 500 miles per hour, Flight 93 raced like a bullet toward the ground. In a flash it was done. The ground shook. A mushroom-shaped cloud of smoke rose above the trees.

Flight 93 had slammed into the ground with terrible force. The airplane was smashed to bits. A scarred, burning crater smoldered in the Pennsylvania countryside.

Forty people were on board, including Mark Bingham, Tom Burnett, and Todd Beamer. No one survived.

The cloud had passed. The unthinkable volume of dust and debris it had carried coated everything—streets, buildings, cars.

Much of Manhattan looked like a war zone. It reminded Rick Leventhal of scenes one might see on the news after a bombing somewhere in the Middle East. He looked out onto the streets. Even the people were covered in dust and grime.

"One hundred ten stories, just … gone," Pat Butler said, shaking his head in disbelief as he looked up at the gaping hole where the south tower should have been. The north tower still loomed over the city. But alone without its twin, it seemed foreign, out of place.

"Where were you when the building collapsed?" he asked a young man. The microphone in Leventhal's hand shook as he waited for an answer. But confusion washed over the man's face. He looked over his shoulder toward the devastation, then back to Leventhal again.

That's when Leventhal realized it. *He didn't know.* Somehow this was the first this man was hearing of the collapse.

"Where have you been all this time?" Leventhal asked him, wondering how someone just blocks from the collapse of a 110-story building could not know.

"In the stairwells," the man answered. "I just got out ..."

*The look on the man's face hit Leventhal hard.* He looked around, realizing that everyone here had a story to tell—all of them powerful. Over the next several minutes, Leventhal conducted interview after interview. He was blown away by the stories he heard. "Living down here, you never see planes that low or that loud," said a man in a sport coat. "We just looked up, and the guy next to me said, 'That's going to hit the Trade Center' ... it looked like a horror movie."

The stories kept coming, one intense account after another. It was all so much to take in at once. Leventhal sometimes found himself at a loss for words. "I don't even know what else to ask you," he stammered. "It's just … horrible."

And so it went on, witnesses to the tragedy telling Leventhal, and the world, what they'd seen, how they felt.

"I can't talk about it …"

"We made it out … we made it out …"

"You see bodies flying out of the sky, and you can't do nothing about it …"

"There's no words to describe what's going on out there …"

A firefighter was describing to Leventhal the chaos of the evacuation when voices interrupted them. People were sprinting down the streets. "Back it up! Back it up!" shouted one man, possibly a police officer.

*What now?* Leventhal thought. Was this madness ever going to end?

Together, Leventhal, Butler, and the firefighter started moving together away from the tower. "Here we go again," he told the camera. He was as rattled as everyone else, but he needed to keep his composure. "Here we go again. I don't know what's going on ..."

That was when an all-too-familiar low rumble echoed through the streets.

The north tower was coming down.

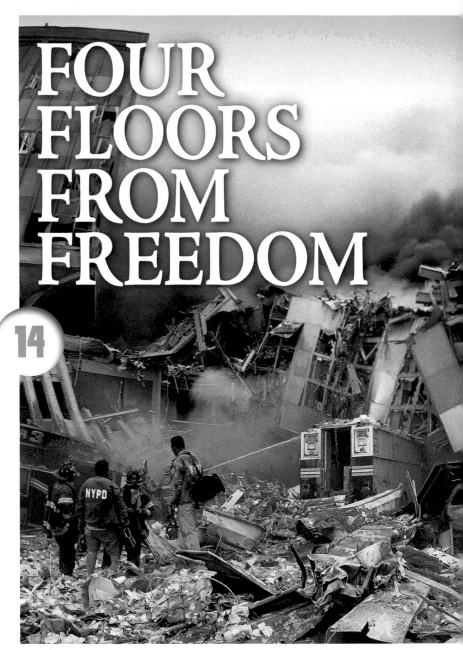

# FOUR FLOORS FROM FREEDOM

14

Fire trucks and other emergency vehicles were crushed under the weight of the collapsing towers.

Josephine Harris had been on the 73rd floor when the plane hit. She'd made it all the way to the fourth floor. Jay Jonas looked at the woman, slumped down on the floor of the stairwell. Sweat drenched her dark skin. She was breathing heavily.

*She's giving up,* he thought to himself. *All this way, just four floors to go, and she doesn't have anything left.* It was heartbreaking.

"That's it," she told them. "I can't go any more."

What was he supposed to do?

He and his men had vowed to stay together. And they had promised to rescue Harris. But everyone knew that the south tower had collapsed, and that building had been hit after this one. Who knew how much longer the north tower could hold out? Jonas shivered. He almost felt like he could hear the clock ticking in his head. Tick … tock. And when it ticked down to zero …

"Open the door," Jonas said. "Find her a chair. Maybe we can get her down that way."

No luck. The fourth floor wasn't an office floor. It was filled with mechanical equipment—nothing of use to Ladder Company 6. Frustrated, Jonas turned back to the stairwell. *OK. We'll just have to drag her.*

*He was reaching to open the stairwell door when it happened. It started as a low rumble. He could feel it as much as he could hear it. The walls and the floor hummed.*

He could guess what was happening. The intense flames had weakened the tower's structure so much that it was collapsing. Stairwell B was in the center of the tower. That meant that right above them more than 100 stories of cement, metal, and glass were cascading down on top of them. The floors were collapsing one by one, crushed by the weight of everything piling up on top of them. BOOM! BOOM! BOOM! BOOM! They could feel each and every floor collapse. They had seconds—only seconds—until that wave reached the fourth floor and smashed them to a pulp.

The roar grew and grew. Above him Jonas could hear the awful wail of steel girders twisting and tearing. Then came a blast of wind as the air in the stairwell was compressed. Matt Komorowski stood on the stairs above the fourth-floor landing. The wind lifted him off his feet and sent him crashing into the wall below.

Jonas closed his eyes and thought of his family as he waited for the weight of the north tower to crush them all.

# DOWN
# COMES
# ANOTHER

**15**

Both towers collapsed, leaving nothing but a
column of smoke in the New York skyline.

# Jan Demczur

"Just breathe deeply," said the EMT, holding an oxygen mask to Jan Demczur's mouth. It was like a war zone, people being treated on the street just blocks from where the north tower still burned. Demczur looked around and removed the mask. He saw people who had passed out, people badly burned. He was one of the lucky ones.

He looked up to where the flames wrapped around the upper part of the north tower. A chill ran down his spine. That's when he noticed the antennas at the top of the building. They were swaying.

He ran. As the building fell, he ran. He ran until he couldn't run anymore, until the sky was blue and the air was clear. He patted himself, his chest, his shoulders, as if to make sure he was really there. To make sure it was really true—he was alive.

*No, no, not again!* Rick Leventhal thought as he scanned the skyline. The sounds of shattering glass, twisting metal, and the rumble of the north tower's collapse covered the street like a blanket of noise. People sprinted down empty streets, searching for shelter from the enormous cloud rising up once again over the city.

This time the debris cloud didn't take them by surprise. Pat Butler held the camera steady as they backed away.

"We need to put it down now," Leventhal told him. "I think we do need to put it down."

But Butler just shook his head and kept filming. He knew that the truck had sheltered them once, and it could do it again. He wanted just a few more moments of footage. Just a little bit more to show the world what this tragedy looked like from ground level.

Finally, as the cloud bore down on them, Butler set the camera down on the sidewalk, carefully aiming it so that it would capture everything. If it survived, the footage would be unbelievable.

The first time, when the south tower collapsed, Leventhal had feared for his life. This time, huddled in the news truck, he was overwhelmed by sadness. *Both towers just gone. Erased from the skyline in a blink.*

"How could this happen?" Butler wondered out loud. Leventhal, breaking into a fit of coughing from all the dust he'd inhaled, had no answers. No one did, at least not yet.

# Jay Jonas

In the remains of the
North Tower, 10:29 a.m.

It was dark. Jay Jonas' lungs
ached from hacking up the dust he'd
breathed in. To his left he heard
moaning, coughing, voices.

The thought struck him all at
once. *I'm alive. We're alive.* It seemed
impossible. Yet ... here he was. The
north tower had crashed down on
top of them, and yet somehow, some
way, he was not dead. It seemed
impossible, but here, right in the
center of the north tower, he'd
found a pocket of safety amidst
the massive destruction.

But he was trapped.

The air was heavy with dust and smoke. All around him, Jonas could hear people struggling to breathe. Just part of the building must have collapsed. He had no way of knowing what still stood or how long it would stay standing. But he had to keep his head.

"Roll call," Jonas hollered with another fit of coughing. He needed to know who was still with him. One by one the men shouted out their names. To his relief and amazement, all of his men were still alive. So was Josephine Harris and a few others who had been on the same level.

A radio crackled as a panicked voice called for help. "Mayday! Mayday! Mayday! This is the officer of Ladder Company 5. I'm in the B stairway on the 12th floor. I'm trapped and I'm hurt bad."

"Cap, did you get that?" asked Sal D'Agostino.

"Yeah, I got it," Jonas replied. He knew the voice. It was Mike Warchola, a good friend. He was just eight flights above them. "Let's go," Jonas said, grabbing a few of his men. "He needs our help."

Debris lay scattered everywhere. Moving through all of it was excruciatingly slow. Jonas stayed low as he crawled over the dust-covered rubble, squeezing through, inch by inch. It reminded Jonas of a stairway in an old abandoned building. You could climb it, but there was no telling how stable it was. It felt like it was always on the verge of collapse.

Jonas made it to the fifth floor, but there the debris was so thick that he couldn't go any farther. He felt almost ill as Warchola sent out another mayday … then a third. There was nothing he could do. Jonas' chest ached as he keyed his radio. He knew that he might be saying good-bye. "I'm sorry, Mike. I can't help you."

He never spoke to his friend again.

As the dust and smoke began to settle, Jonas took stock of his people. Everyone was in surprisingly good shape. A possible concussion here. A separated shoulder there. But nobody was in immediate medical danger. If the building itself didn't suffer more damage, if they could hold on for a rescue, they might all make it.

The emergency bands were lit up with traffic. But eventually, Jonas got a mayday message of his own out. "Hold on, Ladder 6," said a voice. "We'll get you out of there."

"Hey, Cap, what do we do now?" asked Tommy Falco.

"I don't know," Jonas answered. "I'm making this up as I go along."

They had no food or bottled water. They were still choking on dust, and their eyes were red from it, although it was beginning to settle—inches upon inches of it. They could hear the roaring of fires but had no idea how close they were or if they were spreading. Should they be trying to dig their way out? Or should they sit tight and wait for rescue?

"Sit tight," Jonas finally decided. There wasn't much they could do but wait. And so they did as minutes passed … hours. The men explored, looking for anything that could help.

Several of the men were speaking in hushed voices when Jonas' radio finally sounded. "Rescue 3 to Ladder 6," said a voice. "I'm coming to get you."

But it wasn't that simple. As hard as Jonas tried to explain his position, nobody understood.

"How did you get in there … how did you get inside the building?" asked a voice.

That was an odd question. "We just walked in," Jonas said. Then Jonas overheard one rescuer ask, "Where's the north tower?"

That's when Jonas began to put all the clues together. It hadn't been a partial collapse. The entire tower had come down. He could tell the rescuers his location, but they had no frame of reference. The tower was nothing but a pile of rubble, and Ladder Company 6 was somewhere in the middle of it. *They were the needle in the haystack.*

# DAYLIGHT

## 16

Flight 77 crashed into the Pentagon, badly damaging one side of the building.
All 64 people on the plane and 125 Pentagon workers were killed.

# Danielle O'Brien

The Pentagon, about 12:15 p.m.

Smoke was still rising from the gash in the west side of the Pentagon as flight controller Danielle O'Brien stood on a grassy hill overlooking the building. People were everywhere—camera crews, rescue workers, military. She had come to see the scene for herself.

She looked up to the bright blue sky, then back over her shoulder. She could picture it clearly in her mind. A Boeing 757 streaking across the sky over her head, so low that it seemed she could almost touch it.

She closed her eyes. The real target had been the White House. She was sure of it. But the plane had been headed almost straight east—directly into the bright morning sun—and the White House stood beyond a grove of trees.

97

She could almost imagine the scene inside the cockpit. The hijackers had missed their main target and circled. When they had seen the famous shape of the Pentagon building, they'd taken their shot.

She thought back to her final communication with Flight 77—the flight that had done all of this damage. "Good luck," she had told the pilot. Why? She couldn't remember ever saying that to a pilot before. She usually signed off with "good day," or "have a nice flight." Never "good luck."

Why?

O'Brien lingered there on the hill, staring at the shattered Pentagon, replaying the scene over and over in her head. She was exhausted from the day and emotionally spent. Yet she stayed, putting off sleep. She feared what she'd see when she closed her eyes.

Jay Jonas saw it about three hours after the north tower collapsed. A shaft of light stretched down from above. Motes of dust danced and swirled in the narrow column of light ... of daylight.

He was stuck in a stairwell in the middle of the fourth floor, with 106 floors of rubble above, and here he was looking at daylight.

"Huh?" said Tommy Falco, confused. "How is that possible?"

"There's nothing above us, Tommy." Jonas answered. The light told him that rescuers were near. But it also confirmed his worst fear. "That big building doesn't exist anymore."

Minutes passed. The voices outside grew nearer. His men were eager to move, but Jonas was cautious. "We've waited this long. No rash moves now."

All eyes were on the opening above them. Blue sky above. And then … faces. Firefighters. Jonas heard his men let out a collective sigh of relief. Josephine Harris was crying.

It was no easy rescue. They exited the stairwell by a rope, one by one. Jonas and Falco remained behind with Harris until a rescue company arrived with a basket to get Harris out. Only when they knew she was safe did Jonas and Falco leave the ruined north tower.

What he saw when he got out almost brought him to his knees. It was one thing to know that the whole building had collapsed. It was another matter entirely seeing it with his own eyes. It looked like the city had been bombed. Rubble was everywhere. Fires blazed in several nearby office buildings. Explosions rocked the streets as the fire reached the Secret Service arsenal in one of the smaller World Trade Center buildings.

The firefighters of Ladder Company 6 carefully made their way over the rubble field. They were exhausted, bruised, and battered. But they were alive. They had survived.

*How many others had not? Hundreds? Thousands?*

Jonas could only shake his head. He had survived almost impossible odds. But New York City would never be the same. The world would never be the same.

# EPILOGUE

The attacks of September 11, 2001, changed the world. For decades many Americans had felt a sense of separation from global war and violence. That sense of security disappeared in a single dark morning. The attacks served as a catalyst for two wars, one in Iraq and another in Afghanistan. Many also credit the attacks with fostering a new sense of unity and patriotism. Police officers, firefighters, and everyday citizens were celebrated for their acts of bravery.

Some of the people whose actions inspired this tale didn't survive the events of 9/11. But what happened to those who did?

On the 13th anniversary of the attacks, a tribute in light to all those who died rose from the ashes of the towers. Nearly 3,000 people lost their lives on September 11, 2001.

## Nicole Simpson

Her experiences on 9/11 left Simpson in a personal crisis. She struggled to resume her career, and was plagued with nightmares and depression. Simpson wrote a book describing her ordeal and offered help to others coping with similar issues. She has also been active in helping victims of the attacks receive financial benefits.

## Rick Leventhal

Leventhal remains a senior correspondent with Fox News. He has spent time in Kuwait and Iraq covering U.S. Marines at war. He has also covered stories such as the 2005 funeral of Pope John Paul II, the 2010 oil spill in the Gulf of Mexico, and the devastating earthquake in Haiti that same year.

## Danielle O'Brien

Like Simpson, O'Brien was plagued by nightmares after the 9/11 attacks. She has since stayed largely out of the public eye, yet has become an unwitting star amongst 9/11 conspiracy theorists. Some theorists don't believe her descriptions of the airplane match the official account of the disaster.

# Jay Jonas and Ladder Company 6

Jonas and his firefighters were hailed as heroes, making appearances at parades and ceremonies. They stayed in close contact with Josephine Harris, whom the press dubbed the Angel of Ladder Company 6. When Harris died in 2011, Jonas and the men of Ladder Company 6 carried her one last time as her pallbearers.

# Jan Demczur

Demczur and his squeegee became minor celebrities in the years following the attacks. What remains of the squeegee even became part of a Smithsonian exhibit about that day. Yet Demczur also struggled with depression and anxiety. He vowed he would one day return to work, but only on buildings where he could reach every window with a ladder.

# TIMELINE

**SEPTEMBER 11, 2001, 7:59 A.M.:** American Airlines Flight 11 takes off from Boston with 92 people aboard.

**8:14 A.M.:** United Airlines Flight 175 takes off from Boston with 65 people aboard.

**8:21 A.M.:** American Airlines Flight 77 takes off from Dulles, Virginia, with 64 people aboard.

**8:41 A.M.:** United Airlines Flight 93, the last of the four hijacked flights, takes off from Newark, New Jersey, with 44 people aboard.

**8:46 A.M.:** American Airlines Flight 11 crashes into the north tower of the World Trade Center.

**8:47 A.M.:** New York Fire Department forces, including Ladder Company 6, rush to respond to the disaster.

**9:03 A.M.:** Millions watch on live TV as United Airlines Flight 175 crashes into the World Trade Center's south tower.

**9:28 A.M.:** Hijackers break into the cockpit of Flight 93 and take control of the airplane. They assure passengers that they will be all right.

**9:37 A.M.:** American Airlines Flight 77 crashes into the western side of the Pentagon in Washington, D.C., killing 184 people.

**9:57 A.M.:** Passengers aboard Flight 93, aware of the events transpiring on the ground, begin a revolt against the plane's hijackers. Among the revolt's leaders are Mark Bingham and Todd Beamer.

**9:59 A.M.:** The south tower of the World Trade Center collapses just seconds after firefighters are ordered to evacuate the building. At least 624 people die in the tower.

**10:03 A.M.:** United Flight 93 crashes into rural Pennsylvania at more than 500 miles per hour, killing all 40 people aboard. The crash is likely a result of the passenger revolt.

**10:28 A.M.:** The north tower of the World Trade Center collapses. As the collapse reaches the lower level, the mass of debris slows the collapse, leaving a small section of the tower's central stairwell intact. The members of Ladder Company 6, along with several others, are inside the pocket. But at least 1,466 people die in the tower.

**1:30 P.M.:** Rescuers reach the members of Ladder Company 6 in the ruins of the north tower. All of them survive.

# GLOSSARY

**chaos** (KAY-os)—total confusion; anything that throws the world out of balance, such as war

**cockpit** (KOK-pit)—the area in the front of a plane where the pilot sits

**concussion** (kuhn-KUH-shuhn)—an injury to the brain caused by a hard blow to the head

**debris** (duh-BREE)—the scattered pieces of something that has been broken or destroyed

**drywall** (DRI-wal)—a large sheet of inside finishing material; drywall is also called Sheetrock

**evacuate** (i-VA-kyuh-wayt)—to leave an area during a time of danger

**hijack** (HYE-jak)—to take control of an aircraft or other vehicle by force

**mayday** (MAY-day)—a distress signal, usually sent by radio

**revolt** (ri-VOHLT)—a fight against a government or an authority

**terminal** (TUR-muh-nuhl)—a section of an airport

**terrorist** (TER-ur-ist)—person who tries to create fear by killing innocent people or destroying property as a way to gain his or her political or religious goals

# CRITICAL THINKING USING THE COMMON CORE

1. U.S. leaders blamed terrorist leader Osama bin Laden and the group al-Qaida for the attacks on September 11, 2001. Using other texts, explore the terrorists' reasons for the attack and what their goal had been. (Integration of Knowledge and Ideas)

2. All the firefighters from Ladder Company 6 survived being trapped in the fallen tower. How did their personal experiences influence their actions and perspectives on that day? (Craft and Structure)

# INTERNET SITES

FactHound offers a safe, fun way to find Internet sites related to this book. All of the sites on FactHound have been researched by our staff.

Here's all you do:
Visit www.facthound.com
Type in this code: 9781491470794

FactHound will fetch the best sites for you!

# FURTHER READING

Brown, Don. *America is Under Attack: September 11, 2001: The Day the Towers Fell.* New York: Roaring Brook Press, 2011.

Miller, Mara. *Remembering September 11, 2001: What We Know Now.* Issues in Focus Today. Berkeley Heights, N.J.: Enslow, 2011.

Woog, Adam. *The World Trade Center.* History's Great Structures. San Diego: ReferencePoint Press, Inc., 2013.

# SELECTED BIBLIOGRAPHY

"9/11 experiences: A firefighter's story." BBC News. September 8, 2006. http://news.bbc.co.uk/2/hi/talking_point/5303594.stm

"Air Traffic Controllers Recall 9/11." ABC News. October 24, 2001. http://abcnews.go.com/2020/story?id=123822

**Barrett, John.** *Hero of Flight 93: Mark Bingham.* Los Angeles: Advocate Books, 2002.

**Bruinius, Harry.** "A Stunning Tale of Escape Traps its Hero in Replay." *The Christian Science Monitor.* September 9, 2002. http://www.csmonitor.com/2002/0909/p01s02-ussc.html

**DiMarco, Damon.** *Tower Stories: An Oral History of 9/11.* Santa Monica, Calif.: Santa Monica Press, 2007.

**Durso, Fred Jr.** "A Hero's Tale: FDNY Deputy Chief Jay Jonas tells his harrowing story of survival on 9/11." NFPA, June 12, 2012. http://conference.blog.nfpa.org/2012/06/a-heros-tale-fdny-deputy-chief-jay-jonas-tells-his-harrowing-tale-of-survival-on-911.html

**Dwyer, Jim, and Kevin Flynn.** *102 Minutes: The Untold Story of the Fight to Survive Inside the Twin Towers.* New York: Times Books, 2011.

**Jonas, Jay.** "The Entombed Man's Tale." *Times Herald-Record.* September 8, 2002. http://www.thrnewmedia.com/adayinseptember/jonas.htm

**Leventhal, Rick.** "9/11: Never Forget." Fox News. September 11, 2004. http://www.foxnews.com/story/2004/09/11/11-never-forget/

"Remembering 9/11: Incredible Raw Video Shows Rick Leventhal Interviewing Survivors at Ground Zero as North Tower Collapses." Fox News. http://video.foxnews.com/v/1149460964001/remembering-911-incredible-raw-video-shows-rick-leventhal-interviewing-survivors-at-ground-zero-as-north-tower-collapses/#sp=show-clips

**Ross, Brian, and Tom Jarriel.** "Interviews with Air Traffic Controllers Working During the September 11th Terrorist Attacks." ABC News - 20/20. October 24, 2001. http://s3.amazonaws.com/911timeline/2001/abcnews102401.html

**Simpson, Nicole B.** *09/11/01 A Long Road Toward Recovery.* Piscataway, N.J.: Harvest Wealth Media Group, 2011.

**Tate, Bernard W.** "Pentagon Survivors Tell Their Stories," Army.mil. September 14, 2011. http://www.army.mil/article/65490/Pentagon_survivors_tell_their_stories

**Vogel. Steve.** *The Pentagon: A History: The Untold Story of the Wartime Race to Build the Pentagon—and to Restore It Sixty Years Later.* New York: Random House, 2008.

**Vulliamy, Ed.** "Let's Roll …" *The Guardian.* December 1, 2001. http://www.theguardian.com/world/2001/dec/02/september11.terrorism1

# INDEX

American Airlines Flight 77, 11, 106
  hijacking of, 98, 107
Baker, Karen, 58–61
Beamer, Todd, 64–65, 77, 107
Bingham, Mark, 6–9, 51–53, 63–65, 77, 107
Burnett, Tom, 8–9, 51, 53, 65, 77
Demczur, Jan, 21–23, 29–31, 47–49, 74–75, 87, 105
Harris, Josephine, 72–73, 83–84, 91, 100, 105
Jonas, Jay, 24–27, 38–40, 45–46, 70–73, 83–85, 90–95, 99–101, 105
Leventhal, Rick, 67–69, 78–81, 88–89, 104
O'Brien, Danielle, 11, 55–57, 97–98, 104
Pentagon, attack on, 57, 58–61, 97–98, 107

Simpson, Nicole, 13–15, 32–35, 41–43, 104
United Airlines Flight 93, 7–9, 51, 106
  and passenger revolt, 64–65, 107
  crash of, 77, 107
  hijacking of, 52–53, 63–65, 106
World Trade Center
  north tower collapse, 81, 84–85, 87, 88–89, 107
  north tower impact, 14–15, 17–19, 21–27, 33–34, 68, 106
  south tower collapse, 68–69, 71, 72, 74, 78–80, 107
  south tower impact, 37, 39, 41, 58, 106

# ABOUT THE AUTHOR

Author and editor Matt Doeden has written hundreds of children's and young adult books on topics ranging from history to sports to current events. His titles *Sandy Koufax* (Twenty-First Century Books, 2007), *Tom Brady: Unlikely Champion* (Twenty-First Century Books, 2012), and *The World Series: Baseball's Biggest Stage* (Milbrook Press, 2014) were Junior Library Guild selections. His title *Darkness Everywhere: The Assassination of Mohandas Gandhi* (Lerner, 2013) was among the Best Children's Books of the Year by the Children's Book Committee at Bank Street College. Doeden lives in Minnesota with his wife and two children.